Writer

A WRITING NOTEBOOK FROM SKORIAS BOOKS

SKORIAS

© **Skorias 2018**
All rights reserved.

ISBN: 978-1-7323582-2-5

Front Cover Photo © franckito www.fotosearch.com

_____

For more of our books for writers, please visit www.skorias.com

SKORIAS

For more of our books for writers, please visit www.skorias.com

SKORIAS

www.ingramcontent.com/pod-product-compliance
Lightning Source LLC
Chambersburg PA
CBHW052020070526
44584CB00016B/1826